BRACE FOR IMPACT

TEMPLE WEST

AN IN MEDIAS RES BOOK

BRACE FOR IMPACT. Copyright © Temple West 2018. All rights reserved. Printed by IngramSpark.

In Medias Res books may be purchased for business or promotional use. Go to www.ByTempleWest.com and use the contact form to request additional information.

West, Temple.
Brace for Impact / Temple West.

Summary: A collection of poetry concerning depression, family, love, sex, young adults, women, and death.
ISBN 978-0-9983415-9-0 (paperback) — ISBN 978-0-9983415-5-2 (e-book)
[1. Poetry — Non-Fiction.   2. Women Authors — Non-Fiction.]

Book design by Temple West. Cover art by Brian Wooden.

First edition: 2018

10 9 8 7 6 5 4 3 2 1

www.bytemplewest.com

Dedicated to my younger self,
who tried very hard.

FOREWARD

I write poetry when important things — relationships, mostly, or my life — are on the line.

It was not my intention for these to ever be publicly viewed. These poems were emergency measures, emotional first aid, written urgently and with legitimate and immediate stakes. In short, I didn't write them for anyone else — I wrote them to keep breathing. But when you use words this often as a tourniquet, you begin to wonder if there might be something useful to the form.

Whatever your reason for picking up this book, I hope you receive from it what you needed, as I did.

— Temple West

DEATH

Brace for Impact

Six-second slide; southbound suddenly so much closer.
The crunch of paint and concrete kissing,
missing mirror, rubber hissing;
my dad will be so mad, he'll be so mad, it's his car.
Then the ricochet, brake pedal dead against the floor,
flush to the mat, leg hurts from pushing it flat,
turn right, turn into the slide, turn this way or that
but there's cars ahead, stopped dead,
twisted metal corpses in the snow.
The semi sits in fifteen feet, it'll shear the top off my car.
Dad's gonna be so pissed;
we just changed the oil and had the engine —
HIT.

The seatbelt holds. Time rights and
then I see it. Lights,
growing brighter in the black. Twin flames,
eyes boring into mine through the rearview. I've survived,
and they want a crack at the college grad,
want to crack the college grad, crack her car into a million pieces,
snap her spine and smash her jaw and her ribs.
This is the moment I'm going to die. This is how it happens. Shit.
—
—
—
Three heartbeats and it's like nothing you've ever felt before;
you'll drown in your own adrenaline
before the semi can reach you.
Up until the last second you watch him in the rearview,
you watch his lips coming to eat you alive.
Throw up your arms, up over your head;
maybe you'll just shatter your hands,
maybe you'll just shatter your wrists. Maybe, maybe —
HIT.

Like every nightmare you never had.
Like hell. It's like hell, that half-second of suspended gravity,

lifted up, forward, backward, down.
The metal screams, ripped and twisted like rape. A violation;
pushing into my car, pushing my luggage through the back seat.
Skull smacks the window; arm whips the wheel.
After the half-second black-out a flood of facts:
there's no blood, no fractures in the glass.
Not sure why I'm alive, but the surprise passes
and assessment starts:

To the right, gas gushes from a ruptured tank.
If it explodes, I'll be trapped, I'll burn alive.
The Galant is gallant through and through,
hanging on just long enough to power down the window,
then it's out, into the freezing air, shoeless,
socks slipping on the hood of the pickup truck as I make it
away from the potential flames, away from someone else's blood,
away, away, fucking hell, *away*,
to the southbound lanes, to the snow,
away from the slivered glass and the crash and the
sneaking suspicion that you're trapped in *Final Destination*.

Between fight-or-flight there is another instinct:
brace for impact.

Hold on. Hold on and wait for the hit. Take it.
Take it and walk away, physically unscathed.
Wonder how you escaped.
Brace yourself.
Brace yourself and wait.

DEPRESSION

It's Back

Damn the restless shadow,
trips on the backs of heels, this hot, fidgety air;
pushing up on the underside of skin,
stomach gorged with sourceless anger.
God, this burning at the back of throat,
this expletive always on the edge of freedom.
This is the wrath of God in the esophagus,
so barely reigned. This is the hell of the mind,
this is the rabid dog's fury. Powerful,
and then spent.
Drained, can't even sit up straight, can't sigh,
can't cry, can't pray.
It lays there leaden at the center of gravity.
I am too far north. There is not enough sun,
no light overhead to restrict the darkness
to a puddle at my feet.
No, it stretches long, across the street. It follows,
biting at my heels, the hounds of hell.
This is hell, I think.
A taste of hell.

The Quiet

Again you face the quiet of your room,
a hush so deep and still you fear its weight.
Though silence tends to move from such a state,
the moment overwhelms you with its gloom;
stillness that does not breathe or burn or bloom
but lies with heavy hands and breath in bate
to settle on your time and devastate
the attitude you'd carefully assumed.

So face the silence as it stands there still —
go over, sideways, under, or about —
sing softly as you crawl, or loudly shout;
into that void pour sound until you fill
the room with any thought except for doubt
and thus defeat the quiet with your will.

The Demon's Name

There's a little bastard demon with its claws sunk in my back
and his feet have formed a noose, toes twined around my neck
and he jabs me with his tongue and pokes me with his nose
but he blends into my shirt and coat and all my other clothes
so that no one sees the marks that he's left upon my skin
and no one sees the carnage he has caused more deep within
and the demon's name is Chance and when he plays he wins.

There's a little bastard demon with his tongue stuck down my throat
so that half the words I speak out loud get twisted and rewrote,
and he squeezes tight around my chest expelling all my air
so lies come out and fog my sight and lead me toward despair.
And the demon's name is Falsehood and the demon's face is fair.

There's a little bastard demon and his presence seals my fate.
I hate his claws, I hate his grip, I hate his constant weight.
And when I try to shake him off, he loosens round my neck
and slowly creeps back closer when he thinks that I forget.
And the demon's name is Money and the demon deals in debt.

There's a little bastard demon with a silver honey tongue
and he promises me freedom if I carry him along
but I'm paying him in years of life I can't afford to lose
as he whispers saccharine sayings I'm too tired to refuse.
And the demon's name is Promise but he never follows through.

There's a little bastard demon and I want him off my back
but his claws are deeply lodged and he dodges my attack.
And I wonder how my bones would feel if he truly let me be
and I wonder if I'd miss him if he finally let me free.
And the demon's name is Ego and I guess the demon's me.

Fine Fishes

Bum humdinger crap damn it all in a barrel,
fish with no eyes swimming around in the dark,
maybe with one fin cut off, too, and a big buck tooth
so all the other fishes, the fine fishes, the whole fishes,
make fun of the finless fish.
I'm the finless fish.
Where do people come up with the audacity to be whole?

Scattered

Quick trip down memory lane,
Time Hop that ish and curb the disdain you have
for your younger self.
She did the best she could, the best she'd learned to do.
You know better now but it's 10:58 a.m. and you can't move.

You let the demon crawl back up your arm. He looked cute,
this time, and harmless. You thought you could
tame him, you thought you could name him,
keep him like a pet perched up on your shoulder;
little bird cooing back to you.
Go for a walk, you nerd; go for a walk in the light
where the beast can't hide. Tender-fleshed, that one;
it burns when it's bright.
He'll fall right off if you look him in the eyes.

You wish you could sing your feelings,
strike up the band and belt it out
so your voice matched your heart
and your art matched your shout.
But the instrument is half-learned and poorly constructed,
it won't play the way you feel.
Stick, writer, to your pen. To the masses please appeal.

What are vaginas, anyway? Caves, to be flooded.
What an odd organ to possess.

Sex is a mess. Just the whole of it, a wreck.
We so rarely get it right.
too much in tandem, too much to forget.
The brain is a poor conductor, overwhelmed with information.
Wrong station, wrong station, and ah!
Completion.
At least half the train got to its destination.

11:27, this always takes too long. If I were a singer,
I would put it in a song.
Two and a half minutes and then I'd be done.
That's what she said.

So damn wrong.

Insomnia

This will all be over, but not soon;
that's the joy of pain,
how long it lasts,
the thrill of understanding you're about to lose.

Sometimes your limbs don't listen and it proves
that you're not in control
and that's the point of impact,
the sonic blast
that puts you back to sleep.

Gravity

The law that binds all kinds and creeds to earth
is fickle in its rule, and impolite.
It lashes men to dirt, then, out of spite,
releases them aloft, to test their mirth.
If law is thick and thin it has no worth:
stars fall when they refuse to shed their light.
So too must earthborn things be bound up tight
lest tempted to fall up into the night.

Thus gravity is cruel and shows its weight
— perchance to crush the creed out of the man —
just as he overthrows, the law abates
and throws him to the void there to await
the crushing kiss of stars and empty space.

Mute

In a funk,
nothing new.
This, too, shall pass, I can count on that.
But sometimes it all catches up to me
and I let the sadness crash
like glass across my memory
and dance quite carefully through pieces of the past;
little shards of things remembered,
little slices of my history;
the girl who grew up so defensively.
Some part of you just can't believe
that the poison is completely purged,
that you're worth more than you were before,
when you couldn't say a word.

Exchange Rate

Got caught again by the quiet,
wrapped up in silence like a straight jacket;
bound by the sound of nothing at all.
Restless wanderer up and down the stairs
shedding time,
spinning lines about what I'll do if I can find the focus,
little hocus pocus with the words and I'll be good;
I'll be good again tomorrow.
That's the promise, that's the pill I swallow to move on.
I write to beat back the silence,
buy myself another moment, buy space to realign.
I wanted to go out tonight, wanted to get drunk and dance
and lose myself a little in the happenstance but instead I
washed my car and went home and made tea and sat alone
in this room.
And the silence is damning,
pressing in on my endorphins 'til they're cowering
in the corners of my brain,
hiding from my neurons, racking up the joy
of pain.
Flatline, fuckers, I'm here all night.
Staying in, tolerating the sight of my body
sprawled across the bed
sweatpantsed and slippered and sad as sin.
Alone! this picture screams. Alone again.

FAMILY

Product Demonstration

I spent my childhood trying to market myself to my dad,
a product he didn't understand
and never needed.

Occasional Violence

In those moments, I was truly afraid he was going to hurt me.
He never did, but you don't slam someone up against a wall
if you don't want to hurt them,
if you aren't considering it.

Richard

Dad,
your dad just died.
And in the days before
you sat by his side all night,
dozing in fifteen minute bursts
in that hardbacked chair
so if he awoke, alone and confused,
you could bear his weight for him;
keep him whole a little longer.
The second time I ever saw you cry
was at his funeral, attended by so few
at the end of a long
and withdrawn life.
And while you mourned for him,
I mourned for you.

LOVE

Opposites Attract

He was free and reckless and daring
in every way that I was bound and careful and small.

The Law of Equal Exchange

I think of him as purer,
someone I don't deserve
because he has made fewer mistakes.

Rib Cage

He was drunk and I walked him to his room to put him to bed.
He told me he would only go to sleep if I laid down with him,
so I did. When he had his arms around me,
he said he loved me,
trapping me between his chest and his confession.

Parked at Rosedale

So unceremonious:
get out of the car,
walk dry-eyed back to what you were doing before.
He doesn't know what to do with his hands.
He expected something else, not your hair
razed red from the sun through the glass.
He didn't expect to sit above the city on the same road
where you said yes.
The car door is shutting and you're walking
and your eyes are burning but you let it pass
and the car's gone and you're back.
You shake while you wash the dishes.
And later still you sit on your bed with your naked
pillow and bare mattress, waiting for the dryer,
for clean clothes, waiting to put things away,
to put things in order,
to put your clothes in order so you can pull them out
when you need them,
because they're clothes,
because you need clothes.
Waiting for it to sink in.
Waiting for the sound to catch up to your fan.
So unceremonious.
Get out of the car.
Go back to what you were doing before.
With tomorrow irrevocably different.
With tomorrow insanely the same.

Waterfall

Your words are waterfalls, senseless and powerful. They crush beautifully.

Heart

Dissatisfied — already?
The glitter chips off so soon.
The magic wand is just plastic, and blood —
stirred, pumping, and passionate —
is just plasma, protein, and red cells
relieving themselves of oxygen,
blue in the face as they return to the start,
the heart,
one organ among many.

Weed

Shit, this is bad.
Three poems in one night?
Can't quite shake the discontent,
still reeling from that photograph.
Popped up on my feed like that weed that you've plucked
a million times.
You finally think you've got it beat,
then out of nowhere, BAM — it's back:
a photo on your feed,
a weed attack.
This is the source, folks.
This is the bittersweet.
This is the trade-off for intimacy,
the panicked shitstorm of remembering.

So, three poems in one night.
Confusion takes the reigns from certainty,
old things overwhelm the calm.
You don't ever really heal from love:
just bury your face in your arm
and let the panic come.

Carved

Sleep was a fool's dream.
I went looking for ghosts
and found myself surprised to be so haunted.
Funny, how I miss that you once wanted me.
I picture your face and all my careful words freeze,
falling to pieces, into consonants and creases,
and all I can think is, "Shit, please." Shit —
please?
I don't even know what the word means,
it just lingers on the tips of my fingers,
pressed to your face in my memory.

You and the One Before, you carved out your places,
made beams of embraces and painted
my ribs with fingertip traces
so that I can't breathe
without stretching the scars of your faces.

I can't think straight, the mood is muddled.
I would have married either one of you and been wrong,
and that should make your absence lighter —
after all, sir, I'm a writer,
I could run you off the page with half a thought.
But you were made of more than words,
you were burned into my nerves and now
a single thought will conjure you, whether I will it or not.

So goddamn it, love, goodnight,
half a world and out of sight and you're still
carved without consent into my plot.

Shed

I am not so much disappointed
as I am bored with feeling lost.
I want to leave him behind
and replace him with myself.

Aftermath

Unbearable, your new co-adoration,
unbearable your grin, your new tattoos,
the girl you wear like a favorite shirt in all those photographs.
Unkind? Completely.
Unfair? Yes, I confess.
I confess to the absurdity of this
falling in love and
falling out of love and
leaving but not leaving you behind, this
hating my own jealousy.
Self-loathing? Check.
Plots of revenge? Unfortunately, yes.
What male, posed properly, can I slip into a picture you might see
so that you will wonder
if I have forgotten you as effortlessly?
Ah, but no, judgment slips past impulse and I refrain
(think musically, sir, you are a singer after all —
this is the line that I repeat).
I state again: there is no dignity in love. Or if there is,
I have not learned it.
I have not found that kind of love,
not love that passion touches. Passion poisons,
rots, and lingers, staining hearts and tongues and fingers;
acid passion rains on dignity. So where is this wise love,
kind love, that breathes so easily?
Where is the heart that I was promised, the one that understood
the language of these things?
Reason plays no part in this debate,
logic holds no sway. It is old, tired, fickle-footed love
that binds us to our crosses. Sisyphus,
long-rotted, at the top he barely pauses,
just a moment, just to breathe,
as he sees his work fall back into the sea —
so love demands each day our dignity.
Show me better men or better hearts or better ways to love.
I am done paying nightly in poor poetry
and done with petty pain and paltry jealousy.

Perhaps, old friend, it's not the love, or loss thereof,
but the aftermath that's killing me.

Laundry Day

The memories bombard. You washed your sheets today,
and as you're tucking the top one in you remember
that you used to untuck it when he came over
because his feet stuck out over the edge.
But now you can make your bed
and the fact stops you dead;
your heart, like the sheet, limp beneath your head.

Subconscious

It was a cruel dream, and thoughtless,
because it gave me, for an hour, exactly what I wanted.

Amen

Renounce your sighs and tears and tender things.
Proclaim the heart a weak and morbid lie.
Like wishes tied to falling stars on high,
the promises you made were bound with strings,
not forged in solidarity with rings.
So when the truth broke free, you crucified
the beast within your breast that deified
Love, who tricked you into thinking you had wings.

Look there, the girl who always felt too much,
that girl who somehow got it wrong again;
who had within her soul a tender touch;
who, grateful for her heart, cried out amen,
amen, amen, and such and such and such,
again, again, again, again, again.

Cold Call

You called while I was in the hospital.
You called and you were concerned and we were polite
and this is how we are now, between the silences.

Monday

I am weary of hurting, unexpectedly,
in the middle of ordinary things.

Intermission

To the ghosts of our exes —
may they rest in peace
and cease their haunting.
A toast to far-gone faces, then,
and second longings.

Tectonic

The underwater world will shift
and rattle mountains on the rift
and lives will change and I will miss
the way things were before all this.
A stagnant life is sterile, true,
but movement blurs the bird's eye view.
So here I stand all still on pause,
observing you before the cause
that clenched the continent's crooked jaws
and raised and razed the mountain range
and brought about a monstrous change
so that most all familiar things
are nothing more than passing strange.

You're blurred in time
but I remain.

Language

Get me drunk and I'll just want to look at you,
climb on top to get a better view;
trace your knees and your tattoos,
unconscious of the expectation, too focused now for hesitation.
But we're not here to do what people in these situations do.
I'm going to inspect you, investigate the lines,
test the temperature and tone, the density of bones,
compare it all against my literature
and all of the unknowns.
I'm a student and a writer
and your you is bound in words I can't define
(translations, as you know by now, take time) —
what you think we're here to do, that's not my line.
Submit to the inspection, no need for your protection,
we're coming to the thesis of the night.
And when I'm done collecting all the words
you've been erecting, wrap me up in warmth and color
and the languages of lovers
and let dreams rewrite the plot of the playwright.

A Working Definition of Love

Love is patient, love is kind,
it does not hold or break or bind.
It does not envy, it does not boast,
it overwhelms your heart with hope.
It does not seek to serve itself,
it longs to be with someone else.
It is not proud or brought to rage
and only light and life it craves.
It does not memorize past wrongs,
it chases doubt away with songs.
Love loves the truth and hates all fear,
it does not hide but comes to bear
the weight of sadness and despair.
Love is time; time perseveres.

SEX

State of Being

Alluring —
the word you assigned me, a word that doesn't sting
as others do.
Though I've been accused of flirting,
the words are edge-less banter,
no guile or temptation added, no lies intended,
or sensual suggestions, just conversation of a clever sort.
I wonder why my tongue comes off so slick
as if teasing were a trick well-oiled with wear.
I've tried teasing, but my speech gets all impaired.
My true affection is far quieter. If my feelings spoke,
they would chirp in hammered heartbeats,
in hugs held on too long.
My interest would be painted on my cheeks,
easy enough to read,
and far more meek than words. Flirting? I?
Hardly.

But you did not claim I had been teasing,
you assigned to me a state of being.
Therefore take my blush as sign enough:
as opposed to all these other words,
your word leaves room for meaning.

Jungle Party

He was dressed as a skin-tight Avatar,
and I a shipwrecked maiden.
At one point, he told me he needed to change,
and did I want to go with him?
Naive in my camaraderie,
we went upstairs; I stopped to wait.
He asked again:
did I want to come in?
And that's when I was kissed by an alien.
Fun fact: Na'vi has no word for consent.

Desire

Desire is the lowest form of love
and love is at a loss to still our tongue.
But flesh and bone and blood require some
to heat the heart to beat to passion's drum.

And with a lack relations are amiss,
so every touch stains skin with passion's scars.
And lip to lip desire tends to mar
the lasting first impression of a kiss.

I Think We're Missing the Point

He got angry that he couldn't do anything for me, and I got scared every time he tried.

Lovers' Lie

Let's fall in love with love while we are young
and chase the thrill of finding a new face.
We lie and say we do not know disgrace
and count ourselves the lucky ones among
(we say this with our teeth on someone's tongue).
And though we will entreat a warm embrace
it lacks the gentle comfort of the chaste.
We lie and say the kiss has never stung.

What then to do with with sudden shards of shame?
Confide in whom the hint of true regret?
What words skip past lips stained by dying flames
that are not bitter, blasphemed, or offset
by laughter, wit, or other calloused claims
which seem to say, "Say aught, for you'll forget"?

Ah yes, but lips seek out what lips do tend to seek,
with skin the perfect canvas for their touch.
And lo, the rushing shudder may be sweet
and yes, this all may justify the cost —
so goes the clear view rosy in the blush,
thus often lovers in their love are lost.

YOUNG ADULTS

Alice

I was desperate, like any girl,
to grow up.
And staring back behind the looking glass,
I wish I had not been so sure.

Loop

I am there every time he rips you to pieces,
I pick you up and put you back in place.
But every time I do,
your tolerance for pain increases
and my intentions, though well-meaning, are misplaced.

Before

What I wouldn't give to be five again, and ugly, and happy.

The Unrequitables

Watch the city lights from frightened heights,
loose tiles threaten but you're not concerned.
"I dreamed disaster
and you were with me at the end of the world."

"There are no secrets here," you say. "Promise me your
honesty." I promise that I'll try and you nod and it's okay.

We have a case of the unrequitables, raw things
that should not be fulfilled.
"You couldn't frighten me a single bit. Strip
head to toe and I'll chuckle and carry you home.
You are more free than you will ever know."

The cancer grows inside this kid
and you stop a while to carry it with him.

Today would have been something, today
would have been a milestone,
but instead today is grim.
You send your consolations from the road,
and it matters that you've kept the code;
your word that we are friends.

You say I'm not what I say that I am,
but I am because the evidence says so.
I press a question and you respond "I hid
his body in the Yucatan."
I laugh
and know that it is so.

Where I Found You

Pull back for this reprieve,
a leg to lean your cheek against;
shake hollow on the closet floor
and breathe.
You can anchor on to me to reassure yourself
you haven't acted out your plan.
It's okay — or, well, no, it's not,
but you and I are not alone
floating on the closet floor
lost together in your storm.
Your arms lay limp;
there's nothing to say to save you from this.
Pull back, friend,
please don't succumb, don't tread the path that I have gone.
Relief is not worth this
and I won't let you linger long.
Shake hollow on the closet floor
and breathe and grieve and just hold on.

1:42am

I'm twenty-three, impossibly;
the age is sage, it seems.
I know enough of all this stuff
to know I know nothing.

Veritaserum

I was always told that liquor made you truthful.
Get sloshed and spill your beans, whatever they may be.
But the data tells me otherwise,
that lies and truth are equal in inebriation.
Your mind catches on a thought and breathes it into life.
Any thought, the first that comes to mind.
Truth? Perhaps. Lie? Most likely.
Liquor loosens the tongue, but speaks only that which
binds warm fuzzies like science terms, like whatever makes
molecules bond with other molecules.
Electrons and protons, perhaps. I'd have to google that,
and it's beyond me right now.
Liquor pulls good feelings in, spongelike,
magnet-tight, the polarity of which may change
moment by moment.
Do I like your outfit? The liquor does.
Do I like your lips? Liquor says yes.
Warm fuzzies convene on your skin, on your nerves,
vibrating to some intoxicating frequency. You exist
on the surface, suddenly and effortlessly.
So simple. All complexity crystalizes into
this feels good
or
this feels bad.
Liquor is a base equation. A reduction sauce.
Boil us down to feelings and we tell lies and truth
in equal measure
if it will see us through the moment.

Kamikaze

Out, out, damn spot,
burnt your finger on the wick again
flickering, licking the hot spot
as if your tongue can sooth the pain,
but your tongue gets tied into little knots of rage,
so willing to act out
and yet somehow contained.
The words are ready to let fly like kamikaze in their mission.
Fuck all those delicious lies of omission.
But you can't let them loose,
you can't partition your will and your violence
so you're silent
and the words stay grounded on your tongue,
lungs drowning in the oxygen.

Let's try again:
take a breath, spit it out, but the rage disappears
and the flame's gone out
and the hot spot has cooled and the words are fooled
into thinking they're not needed;
close your lips and brood.
For such a strong muscle, your tongue trips up often,
tapping at the nails in the conversation's coffin.
Oh, now you've got nothing left to say?
Stay silent, fine, keep it all inside;
sounds like a stellar plan to get your way.
That's missing the point, though, it's not about winning,
it's beginning and ending with the truth.
So you say a few prayers and magically, POOF,
no aid comes from heaven and the circumstance stays
as it has always and will always remain:
you're still stuck with nothing but rage on your lips
and the knowledge that things don't much change,
they persist.

The Poet

I took Spanglish to heart and refused to cry
so my inner kid just gave up and died.
And that's when it changed, that's when I shut down.
I grew fond of using "fuck" as a gerund for nouns.
The rhythms grew simpler, the rhymes grew coarse.
My artistic voice grew artistically hoarse.

And then this poet got on stage and changed the game for me,
he changed the way that words could say the things
that I could never say to the people who were hurting me.
Disconcertingly, his words flew past,
complex and dense, alive with alliteration,
and when he finished and took a breath
I finally saw what he could see:
that words were whatever we asked them to be.

I was too big to be passive but too small to fight
and it was right, somehow, it was poetic
that poetry gave me power
over impossible odds and physical force,
against divorce,
against a course I could not swim against.
I could break
the lines,
I could force them to flow,
they would grow and take on a life of their own,
but they'd always come from me, like the children
I swore I'd never bear, like the air from my lungs:
mine, and not mine.

Thine is the kingdom and the power,
and mine is the misery, the cycle of despair.
The Lord's Prayer may soothe some
but I was never one to be uplifted by the holy.
I was angry, and the cadence tore into my soul
and the rhythm made me want to rip my sackcloth off
and run naked through the Bible so the words might stick to me

in ways I'd understand.
The divine was made manifest in the Word, in a book,
and while that milk and honey may have tasted sweet
in someone else's tongue,
I only saw the brittle bones of thoughts that were once beautiful.
And the poet, six years ago? He had the taste of holiness.
He could express the torment of a loving god,
the anguish of free will.
For those who were still enough to listen,
he could bring peace in a way the gospel never did.
So this one's for him — whatever his name is —
the poet who gave me new views of God,
the one whose words taught my own to forgive.

The Long Way Through

I cannot hold the hearts of those whose hands ache with rage,
I cannot mend the ones who crave disaster. Something must break.
Sometimes that's just the way of things.
And so I wish to kiss the broken brows of the beaten down,
but peace is a conclusion you can't skip to.
The rage we are slaves to must play out.
We must exhaust the anger
until we understand.

Self [Love]

Unique and special, every child,
groomed and coached on how to smile,
painted, sprayed, plucked, shaved, and tanned;
bait to catch a wealthy man.
Husband? Farce! A business deal.
Sex and youth, get down please; kneel.

No, no, too dark. Rewind, I'll change my spiel.

We seem, from birth, to learn things upside down.
Unleashed, untrained, we burn through childhood
taught not that what we do is right or wrong
but that we're each of us a god (and well renowned),
our words alone are law, our views profound.
Demanding praise and to be understood,
at every "No" we claim our victimhood.
Not knowing how to walk, we fuck around.

Our fault? Perhaps. It doesn't matter now.
We're learning our true place among the stars.
Not skilled or disciplined, but proud,
it's Tuesday and we're shit-faced at our bars.
Slow-clap for looking svelte and tres highbrow.
Addicted principessas, drunken czars,
we're kings of self-indulgence, well endowed;
we mutilate ourselves to prove we're scarred.

Though now we see the gold gleam lose its lust,
our bodies wracked with heaves from needing more,
we don't expect a savior at the door;
no angel white could make us more nonplussed.
We never try to stop and say, "Enough,"
And thus we learn to love our own disgust.

[Young] Adults

Boxes again, filled with the things that bring meaning.
Full, fit to bursting with your life —
take it, then, shake it, watch the colors run kaleidoscope;
this is why we run because the happy colors start to choke
our throats, but we're adults and so we swallow and move on
and get jobs that we hate, and we learn to love to hate,
and we take our money and we celebrate and oh,
we're poor again, eating rice and ramen. Amen to carbohydrates
and fast food and the substances that alter mood
and the friends who take the plunge with us and swear and fuck
and sweat with us.
We don't understand yet that we are wrong,
that we are so far gone in our habits and mistakes.
Prudence is a virtue no one can digest
so we move on and climb up and go down and digress.
This is a mess, this age, and so distressing; we try and pull a page
from our parents' books, but look how they turned out.
The lie of youth is that it has a better truth,
and ignorance isn't wisdom it's just sad. We get so mad,
sometimes, that we don't understand things better,
that these are the choices that we have
and none of them seem right
and we cannot reconcile what we see and what we wish we had
the brains to fight for. We wish we had friends we would die for,
but then there's just the friends we get high with and sleep with
and lie to and cheat with.
We move constantly and want more than what we know;
we are restless and heartfelt and bitter and sore.
Move over, Godzilla, 'cuz here comes the roar —
oh wait,
nevermind,
now we're bored.

HUMANS

Inhuman

We are born as close to innocence as we will ever get
and break down from there, until — at the end —
we rightly question our humanity.

Surely humans couldn't fall this far.
We must be something else
entirely.

WOMEN

Kyle Next Door

You had roller blades, shiny hard wheels
fresh from the factory with that new pool-plastic smell.
You were rich, a Nintendo 64,
a personal computer with Rollercoaster Tycoon,
a twelve inch television right there in your room.
We played soldier and nurse and I'd sew you back up,
tapping your arm wound with my needle fingers.
You were a latchkey kid
and you showed me the rock that was not a rock
and the way to get into your house.
You had six-inch sharks in a tank in your kitchen.
You had parents that were never home.
I guess you were my first kiss, when I was six.
Crouching in my dilapidated fort, you'd demand my lips
if I wanted to play with your toys (which I did).
I'd stand still while you held me in your grip.
Mouth to mouth, payment was due.
And then that final memory of you,
inviting me up to your room.
The first man, at seven, who taught me
I was a thing to be consumed.

Open Season

I'm not ready to jump in again,
not ready to relive again
the closeness of being,
of being seen and seeing,
of leaning on the frame of me + you.
But I'm a One now, I'm a Single, re-learning how to mingle
(good God, how does one mingle?),
I'm a texter, very lingual,
but when it comes to real world suitors, Lord,
I haven't got a clue.
Not true, I'm just not ready
to be told that I am sexy,
that I'm pretty, that they'd bed me,
that their balls are nicely blue.
Could I be a dear (a pretty deer)
and handle one or two?
I'm not ready for more kisses,
no more moans, that's not what bliss is,
my God, my heart is running out of room.
She's going stag? It's open season,
shoot to kill, it stands to reason
the time is ripe, she'd be just perfect to consume.
She must be caught, the only question is by whom.

If you ask, I will decline
because the fact remains the same, good sirs,
the game has been unkind
and the hunters must be taught they're out of line.

Really, Really Stream of Conscious...ness

Tacos for dinner, you know that means margaritas.
Lightweight Champ, bit tipsy, little lippy,
tequila makes the reservéd girl quippy.
So let's do this shit, let's dance.

Romance. Am I right? It's a thing
we're losing. I was not perusing Tinder
because that shit is not amusing. Great rhyme, right?
Roll with it, getting the stream tight, getting the words rolling,
shouldering the weight of the day, adjusting the pack
tracking toward a conclusion, a theme at least —
hey, hey, she speaks. She does that,
she's a writer.
Bit tighter, there we go.

Yep, lonely. Yep, stony on occasion. Self-imposed this and
that, clickety-clack, those heels in the office, the only woman
in the den. Old-boys talking kids and wives, I'm at my desk
scripting swords and spies, keyframed supernatural eyes,
old as dirt, this drive. Need a new one? Nah,
it's spinning still, not an FTL, but fuck it,
bits and bytes get you here to there,
bear with me while I boot the program that lights up worlds.
Hurl your thoughts onto the screen,
tutorial that shit 'til you understand,
keep trying 'til you've caught the thing you sought
right between the ease in and ease out, between the
nays and naughts;
you've figured out the magic. Figured out you
have what it takes to
craft whatever your brain shakes loose when it
thinks of beauty and wonder, seducing you with
power. It's a program,
you're a god. Charge one-fifty an hour,
the plug ins make you fired up. Your only regret now is,
at two days to twenty-seven, you wasted too much time
wondering if you were enough for him.

That was the wrong question. Should've wondered if you were
grabbing your life by the scruff of the neck
for the wonder, for the glory, for the awe, hell it's fucking beautiful,
this life. You should've tried harder, fought smarter,
for more time.
More time to learn it, all the pieces that make up who you are.
A thousand stories, but not enough of you to write them.
You hope that after death
is time.
You hope that's the gift. To grow on and on and —
Martin and Jordan, how did you lash yourself
to a single tale, spread out over thousands of pages?
How did you find the strength to restrict yourself to one world,
like a marriage bound in vows of loyalty?
I cannot be so contained. The stories burst against the chains,
praying for my hands to be swifter than my brain.
Good rhyme? No. It's strained.
I digress, but the point remains:
let's dress our lives in the delights of labor,
let's give ourselves to savoring our work.
Let us live according to our calling,
where heart meets woe meets grace meets longing.
Let's let our lovers rest and fill our lives with better tenderness.
Let's speak more softly.
Let's live as though our lives depended on belonging
to something more
and something better
than just prolonging death. Mourn? Yes.
Mourn for the wasted days
and wasted breath.
Two days to twenty-seven and I'm just now stretching out to reach
for all of it.

ACKNOWLEDGEMENTS

Thank you, Mom, for always leaving books on your nightstand so I could steal them when you weren't looking.

Thank you, Mr. Bratt, for reading my entire 50-page epic poem in high school. I finally understand the energy and time sacrifice you made.

Thank you, Rachel, for taking me to my first Round at the Abbey, and for so many other things.

Thank you, Nathan, for cultivating the Round. It changed my life.

TEMPLE WEST

I've never been much good at restricting myself. I've been told by various professionals to pick a genre and a format and stick with it. I've been told to market myself exclusively as one thing or another, so as not to confuse audiences or agents or networks or publishers. I understand the reasoning behind this.

But here is the simplest definition I can give: I am a writer. A screenwriter, a novelist, a poet, a lyricist, an essayist, even occasionally a journalist. Language has been the scaffolding upon which I have built everything else. Take away the words and I am reduced to a husk of goop and flesh.

Whatever medium is ours, we are all asking to be understood. So take the words as you will, knowing they are a translation of my self offered up earnestly.

www.bytemplewest.com

www.ingramcontent.com/pod-product-compliance
Lightning Source LLC
Chambersburg PA
CBHW070438010526
44118CB00014B/2098